I Can't Make a Flower

a Flower

Margaret Spivey

Illustrated by Diana Catchpole

Judson Press ® Valley Forge

I can't make a flower,
but God can!

God makes beautiful, sweet-smelling
flowers.

I can't make a flower,
but I can plant a seed or bulb!

If someone helps me put it in the ground, I can water it and wait for it to grow.

Thank you, God, for flowers, and thank you for things I can grow.

I can't make a tree,
but God can!
God makes trees grow tall and
strong and shady. Sometimes
they give us fruit!
I can't make a tree,
but I can grow!

Every day I grow a bit bigger
and reach a bit higher.

Thank you, God, for trees,
and thank you that I am
growing big and strong!

I can't make a sun,
but God can!

God made the sun round
and golden and warm. Everyone's
happy when the sun shines!

I can't make a sun,
but I can smile!

My smile makes people
feel happy and warm, just
like the sun.

Thank you, God, for the
sun, and thank you for
smiles.

I can't make a moon,
but God can!

God made the moon big and round and silvery white, shining in the dark sky.

I can't make a moon,
but I can blow a bubble!

The bubbles I blow are round and shiny,
just like the moon.

Thank you, God, for the moon,
and thank you for bubbles.

I can't make a star,
but God can!

God made the stars that
brighten up the dark sky –
thousands of tiny stars.

I can't make a star,
but I can laugh!

When people laugh, their eyes
twinkle like the stars.

Thank you, God, for stars, and
thank you for letting me laugh.

I can't make the wind blow,
but God can!

God makes the wind blow through
the trees. They wave their
branches in the air.
I can't make the wind blow,
but I can dance!

I wave my arms and hands and nod my head, just like the trees.

Thank you, God, for the wind, and thank you that I can dance.

I can't make thunder,
but God can!

God makes the thunder tell us:
'Look out! It's going to rain –
you'll get wet!'

I can't make thunder,
but I can clap!

I can clap to say, "Here I am!"
I can clap to say, "That's
wonderful!"

Thank you, God, for
thunder, and thank you that
I can clap.

I can't make a rainbow,
but God can!

God makes a rainbow of lovely
colors that curves across the sky
on rainy days.

I can't make a rainbow,
but I can color!

I can color a book with crayons or paints and make lots of pictures. I can brighten up a rainy day, too!

Thank you, God, for rainbows, and thank you for my coloring.

I can't make an animal,
but God can!

God makes lions and
tigers, puppies and
kittens, elephants –
everything!

I can't make an animal,
but I can make noises!

I can roar like a lion, bark like a dog, and meow like a cat.

Thank you, God, for animals, and thank you for the noises I can make!

I can't make a bird,
but God can!

God makes birds that fly
and whistle and sing.

I can't make a bird,
but I can sing a song!

I can sing for fun, and I can sing
songs that say thank you to God.

Thank you, God, for the birds,
and thank you that I can sing.

I can't make a fish,
but God can!

God makes fishes that swim and splash in
the rivers and seas.

I can't make a fish,
but I can splash!

I can splash when I swim or step
into a puddle. It's good to feel water
squishing through my fingers or under my
boots!

Thank you, God, for fishes,
and thank you for splashes.

I can't make a hill,
but God can!

God makes hills so that we
can climb to the top and see
faraway places.

I can't make a hill,
but I can climb!

I can climb a hill,
up the stairs, into bed, into a lap!

Thank you, God, for hills,
and thank you that I can climb!

I can't make a world,
but God can!

God made the world full of lovely
things – flowers, birds, mountains and
trees. God made the sun, moon, and
stars as well!

I can't make a world,
but I can help God to make the
world beautiful.
I can smile and laugh, sing and
dance, and clap my hands.
Thank you, God, for the world,
and thank you for making me!

Published in Great Britain by Scripture Union ® 1994

North American Edition ® 1994
Judson Press, Valley Forge, PA 19482-0851

Library of Congress Cataloging-in-Publication Data

Spivey, Margaret.
    I can't make a flower/by Margaret Spivey; illustrated by Diana Catchpole. –
North American ed.
        p. cm.
        ISBN 0-8170-1212-5
        1. Creation – Juvenile literature. 2. God – Juvenile literature. 3. Gratitude –
Religious aspects – Juvenile literature. [1. Creation. 2. God. 3. Gratitude.]
I. Catchpole, Diane, III. II. Title. III. Title: I can't make a flower.
BL226.S85 1994
231.7'65–dc20   94-11793

Printed and bound in Singapore.